CW01432366

SIGNIFICS AND LANGUAGE

MACMILLAN AND CO., LIMITED
LONDON · BOMBAY · CALCUTTA
MELBOURNE

THE MACMILLAN COMPANY
NEW YORK · BOSTON · CHICAGO
ATLANTA · SAN FRANCISCO

THE MACMILLAN CO. OF CANADA, LTD.
TORONTO

SIGNIFICS
AND LANGUAGE

THE ARTICULATE FORM OF OUR EXPRESSIVE AND INTERPRETATIVE RESOURCES

BY

V. WELBY

"All life therefore comes back to the question of our speech, the medium through which we communicate with each other. . . . The more it suggests and expresses the more we live by it—the more it promotes and enhances life. Its quality, its authenticity, its security, are hence supremely important for the general multifold opportunity, for the dignity and integrity, of our existence."—HENRY JAMES.

UNIV. OF CALIFORNIA

MACMILLAN AND CO., LIMITED
ST. MARTIN'S STREET, LONDON
1911

VIPU

J 540
W43
1911
MAIN

DEDICATED

TO

MY MANY KIND SYMPATHISERS AND FRIENDS

AND TO

ALL THE YOUNG WORLD

.

PREFACE

SIGNIFICS may be briefly and provisionally defined as the study of the nature of Significance in all its forms and relations, and thus of its working in every possible sphere of human interest and purpose. But the fact that this study is completely neglected even in education renders a fully satisfactory definition difficult at present to formulate. The interpretative function is, in truth, the only one in any direct sense ignored or at least casually treated. And yet it is that which naturally precedes and is the very condition of human intercourse, as of man's mastery of his world.

In reading the following pages two things must throughout be borne in mind.

First, that the plea for Significs can only as yet be written in that very medium—conventional language—which so sorely needs to be lifted out of its present morass of shifting confusion and disentangled from a rank growth of falsifying survival ; and second, that the present writer has no claim to make that plea as it should be made by those who, even as things are, could do it far better justice.

Readers must also be warned that the book is not a continuous Essay, still less a systematic Treatise. It consists of a selection made from a great number of short papers, written over a course of years, and always without any view of publication. Some of these papers were intended to explain to correspondents and friends the writer's position with reference to language ; and others, again, were the form in which the writer recorded for personal use some new aspect or way of putting the matter, as it suggested itself. It has been thought that a selection of such Papers, of which these are but a few examples arranged and modified as seemed advisable, would serve to indicate some directions in which the theme of earlier writings could be developed.

In the Appendix will be found a small supplementary selection of a different kind ; that is, representative expressions of the needlessly narrow limitations and positive obstructions of language which are now beginning to be widely felt.

It must finally be borne in mind that the suggestions here offered constitute little more than an elementary sketch of a vast subject. Even as contributed by the writer, there is abundant material for succeeding volumes, showing the practical bearing of Significs, not only on language but on every possible form of human expression in action, invention, and creation.

I now have to acknowledge my debt of gratitude to those who have helped me to make possible this suggestion of a central need and its true fulfilment.

In a previous stage of the work—that represented by *What is Meaning?*—I had to return thanks for the ungrudging help of a long list of distinguished advisers, who were also friendly critics. But of course I had no excuse for again troubling those who had so generously responded to my first appeal.

In this case I have to repeat my gratitude to Professor Stout, to whom I owe more than I can express. I must also warmly thank

Dr. Slaughter and Mr. Greenstreet, and a few others who have indirectly helped on the work or encouraged the worker.

My main thanks, however, in the present undertaking are due to Mr. William Macdonald, without whose expert aid I could not, from somewhat failing strength, have faced so formidable a task.

V. W.

I

THERE are probably many who dimly realise, and would provisionally admit, that our present enormous and ever-growing developments of mechanical power and command are there to be interpreted in terms of psychology. This must presumably affect not only the very minds which are conceiving and applying them to such tremendous and apparently illimitable purpose, but also the thinkers concerned with the mental sphere itself, its content, and its range.

We may thus suspect, if not actually infer, that human thought also is on the threshold of corresponding developments of power,—developments to which the "new birth" of scientific method in the nineteenth century was but the prelude and preparation. If, indeed, we deny this conclusion, or dispute this assumption, we may effectually hold such a development in arrest —or risk forcing it out in unhealthy forms— just as, three hundred years ago, the spirit of scientific discovery was fettered and retarded on the verge of its great career of achievement. The explanation is in part, if only in part, the same now as it was then. For in the pre-Baconian age the study of phenomena, the inquiry into " the causes of things," was not more inhibited by theological prepossessions and denunciations than by the dominance of an intellectual nomenclature which ruled reality out of the universe and confidently took its place in all disquisition or discussion upon Man and Nature. The forward step taken was largely the result of a breaking of the barriers created by traditional terminology, a pushing aside of fictitious formulas, and a coming directly into the presence of things in order to learn whatever they had to say " for themselves "—and for the Whole. All the conditions — especially the supreme condition, an urgent need—are now existent for a second and similar forward step, but upon another plane and to higher purposes. For the fresh advance which now seems imminent, as it is sorely needed, should be no mere continuation of the Baconian search, the accumulation of data for a series of inferences regarding the properties of the material system as usually understood, but rather the interpretation, the translation at last into valid terms of life and thought, of the knowledge already so abundantly gained. While man fails to make this translation—to moralise and humanise his knowledge of the cosmos, and so to unify and relate it to himself—his thinking is in arrears, and mentally he lags behind his enacted experience. That we in this age do lag behind, and that we have thus far failed to achieve a great and general act of translation, is a loss chiefly due to our unanimous neglect to understand Expression, its nature, conditions, range of form and function, unrealised potencies and full value or worth. And therefore the first message of what is now to be named Significs [1] is that we must amend this really inhuman fault ; that we must now study Expression precisely as we have long been studying " Nature " and " Mind " in the varying ranges of both these terms.

We must do this ; for until we do it, not merely metaphysical theory but natural fact, as well as moral and social valuations and aims, must continue to be perpetually misinterpreted because mis-stated. Great tracts of experience, direct and indirect, remain without an ordered vocabulary or notation—and better none than those which many others have—exactly as great

[1] For a definition of this term see the *Oxford Dictionary*, the *American Dictionary of Philosophy*, and the *Encyclopædia Britannica*, 11th edit.

regions of natural fact remained without recognition and without name until man almost suddenly discovered that he had been looking for the whats and hows and whys of the world he lived in in the wrong direction and by the wrong method. At last he saw his true way—that of faithfully interrogating Nature, and rigorously testing his reading of her answer —and rich has been the reward of following it loyally. But the proper complement of this wonderful step forward, its very issue, must be the opening up of another true way hitherto untrodden. It must be the recognition and use of a method, a mental procedure and habit, enabling us to perceive the treasures of truth, the implications of reality, that even now are only hidden from us by our contented subjection to the tyranny of misfitting Expression,—Expression, of course, of all kinds, but mainly expression in language, taken in its ordinary sense.

Our punishment here is that some of the most intimate and homely as well as important and significant forms of experience, some of the plainest facts and most real existences in the world, remain 'unknowable' in the sense of being 'unspeakable' and therefore 'unthinkable' in any now fitting sense. As a fact, however, as we are constantly, though unconsciously witnessing, we can think in an embarrassed and hindered way much more than language, in the forms which social and other conventions have imposed upon it, allows us satisfactorily to express. In all thoughtful and able writing we continually meet with signs of a sense of shortcoming in expressing given conceptions : but whatever the failure, the conceptions are there.

In these cases we do note the inadequacy of language to serve. In others, and more frequently, we note the fear of its great fund of fallacies. We constantly find scattered throughout the text of every thoughtful treatise what are essentially footnotes of protest or warning, made needful only by the universal attitude of a reader who has never been trained to demand new and fruitful ideas, and to be ready to welcome new and suggestive modes of setting these forth. For lack of such training, the reader persistently reads the old prepossessions into the new statement of truth, and so merely works over, *ad nauseam*, the bare and dead tissues of used-up thought, once living and active, now mummied.

Our language has been full of life, since all its similes, all its associations, like all its assumptions, were once in perfect accord with

the current conceptions of ' nature,'—our own
nature included, — and with our ideas of
' motion, matter, and mind.'   But now, just as
the forms of expression called social convention
and common law no longer fit our knowledge
of the biological and psychological facts of life,
are confining us to stunted and mean conceptions
of morality, and are causing cruel travesties of
justice whether social or legal ; just as the form
of expression called music puzzles and baffles,
while it fascinates us and leads to barren controversy ;[1] just, indeed, as all current forms of
expression, except, perhaps, the fast growing
modes of mathematical symbolism tend to do
this—so the form of expression called linguistic,
our phrase and our word spoken or written,
betrays us daily more disastrously, and atrophies
alike action and thought.

[1] See Edmund Gurney's "Power of Sound" and Gehring's
"Expression in Music," *Phil. Rev.*, July 1903, and many other
recent Essays on Music.

II

APPARENTLY we suppose that the 'gift' of
language is like the 'gift' of a nose, entirely
(as to its position and office) outside the scope of
our modifying control.   And it is true that we
cannot invert our nose, or give it four nostrils, or
present it with the power of hearing or sight.
Neither, indeed, can we develop it into an organ
of (at present) transcendent smell, no, nor even
restore to it its pristine and sub-human privileges.
But all this only shows that we had better leave
off talking of 'gift' when speaking of language.
Rather, we have painfully earned the possession
of speech by learning to control and order
the sounds producible by our evolving larynx,
and by continuously, consistently, arduously,
purposively developing the complexities of the
resulting system of vocal signs.   In doing this
we have evolved and developed syntax and
prosody and much else that the philologist,
orator, or poet can expound to us, or use to
influence our feeling and action.   The point is,

that just when the need of adding consensus to a so far accomplished control was most urgent, and its neglect most certain to be disastrous to our intellectual fortunes; just when a high civilisation and what we call the modern era of discovery and its reaction on philosophical thought and practical life set in, we began to lose more and more the very idea of a social control, and of power to direct the development, of the most precious of all our acquirements, that of articulate speech.

I can never forget the amazement I felt when I first began my study of philology and linguistics and the origins of language, and realised this fact and its full significance. The writers one and all treated language, not as you would treat muscle, as a means of work to be brought under the most minute, elaborate and unfailing functional control, but as you might treat some distant constellation in space and its, to us, mysterious movements. We might describe such a heavenly object and then lay down what seemed to be the conditions of its existence and activities. We might point out precedents; possible origins; possible destinies; possible effects on other systems, including our own. But we should remain consciously and profoundly helpless to modify in the most

trifling degree, or in any sense, its career and its
perturbing or contributory powers.

It does not seem to have dawned upon any
one, either specialist or ' lay,' what a tremendous
absurdity all this way of regarding language
involves.   No wonder, however, when so far
no writer on the subject of language has ever
reminded us with any emphasis, still less with
the needed impressiveness, that the one crucial
question in all Expression, whether by action
or sound, symbol or picture, is its special pro-
perty, first of Sense, that in which it is used,
then of Meaning as the intention of the user,
and, most far-reaching and momentous of all, of
implication, of ultimate Significance.

When the cardinal importance of all forms
of Expression, but pre-eminently of language,
has been impressed on a coming generation
from its very infancy, that generation will rise
and resume an efficient direction of its own
greatest acquisition.   We have done, we are
doing this with extensions of muscle and
sensation ; with Machine, Instrument, and
Apparatus.   We must do it with a greater than
these in any ordinary sense of the words.   We
must do it with the greatest of extensions, that
of natural cry into articulate and reasoned
speech.   And this, not merely as a question of

redressing and giving better finish to a frame-work, or of improving on conventional grammar, prosody, and so forth, but as the development of an expansive and, so to say, organic power as yet only in embryo. And surely it is evident that no rhetoric and but little imagination are needed to convey an idea of what may be hoped for when this result has been at last, through a significally sane education, brought about. It is indeed the plainest of common-sense that concentration upon the value of all Sign, and the effective co-ordination of all our means of enhancing and realising this to the very utmost, must bring about a forward step, one of the greatest Man has ever made and the world has ever seen.

III

Iᴛ is true that we sometimes seem to lay claim to such control, as when we praise an orator or writer for his "command of language." But there is, in fact, no such command. There is an amazing and an even contented subserviency and helplessness, leading too often to inexcusable defect or deviation of sense.

We conceive that the nearest approach to the mastery which is our true birthright was achieved in what we call the classical era. And we are still living in an almost literal sense on its legacy. But the spirit of its conquests and domination is lost, and with that the lesson of its effective greatness. To a large extent, though in varying degrees in different races, we avail ourselves of attitude, gesture, and tone by these primitive means, shared in varying (and often to us imperceptible) modes and degrees by the whole organic world. But our speech constantly mocks us and our interest. This is not the fault of Expression itself in any form, least of all of articulate expression, that loyal creation and

unfailing servant of Man, ready and untiring as
inexhaustible, waiting only for our recognition,
and for that commanding guidance which only
in the most important case of all we have failed
to apply.   No : it is our own fault.

The idea that such neglect and helplessness
are inherent in the case is peculiarly inept.
Articulate expression is the elaborated and trans-
figured form of attitude, gesture, and tone ; and
more yet, of the marvellous skill of hand directed
by creative brain, of the inventor and worker,
the representative of imagination and reason.
Why do we only 'invent' mechanical instruments, when the greatest instrument of all lies
in comparative neglect, as a thing with which
we have nothing to do beyond doing what we
can with it as it is ?   Speech gives our 'mind,'
our thought, our conception ; it conveys our
knowledge, describes our difficulties, records our
endeavours and our successes or defeats, warns
or encourages, notifies objection, refutes error,
exposes blunder or inaccuracy ; and finally
explains and enables us to apply the principles of
achievement of any kind.   Having the offered
service of such a power as this, why should we
slight or disregard its promise, or be content
with anything less than its highest efficiency,
which will also be ours ?

IV

THE most important elements of experience are distinction and unification, comparison and combination — analysis and synthesis. We first analyse what is called a confused manifold, really a generic or 'given' manifold. Then we synthetise what we have distinguished to the uttermost. If the result were an actual complex, say a system of motions, particles, or masses, we should take care not to muddle up the constituents. We might pay too obviously dear for that ! But in language this elementary rule of practical or even rational procedure is violated by our pernicious misuse and perversion of one of the most splendid of all our intellectual instruments, namely, the image or the figure ; the image which is not merely the analogue, but in a broad and true sense the linear descendant of the retinal image indirectly giving us the immediate reality of the ' material world '—of perception.

Now we do know the danger of actual

optical illusion and of delusion arising from
disease of mind or body. We do understand
that if we supposed we saw solid earth beyond
a cliff-edge, and walked over it, we should be
killed ; and we infer this, although we had not
deliberately realised or examined it. But we do
not see that we are killing or injuring ourselves
mentally by tumbling down logical precipices or
into metaphorical pits and so on, because of the
traps set by false mental images in language.
Upon the presumptions suggested by these dis-
tortions of image we too often act, and in our
thinking are continually influenced by them.
Therefore it is hardly an exaggeration to say
that within the realm of speech our procedure
is that of the insane.

Hence the divisions, the antagonisms between
men of goodwill. Hence the unsound pessimism
and the equally or more unsound optimism which
distort our interpretation of the world.

Hence, indeed, the 'insoluble problem,' even
that of ' Life' itself, though if really a problem
it must of course be soluble. If we could but
see this ; if our insanity of mental image could
be cured or, rather, averted in childhood ; if
our imagery were rectified ; then ideas would
emerge which now are killed in the germ.
Then conceptions would be formed which now

never come to the birth. Then mental organisms would come to perfect maturity, which now are stunted and deformed. Then beauty, dignity, grace of which as yet we have less than a possible measure, might be hoped for.

V

THROUGH the prevalence of misfitting imagery, which continually misrepresents the real aspects and relations of things, and warps our reasoning as well as our vision of the world, we are really living in what is (comparatively speaking) a kind of lunacy, a state of general illusion, 'materialising' here and there into definite delusions about which we are controversial and emphatic. We need a linguistic oculist to restore lost focussing power, to bring our images back to reality by some normalising kind of lens. Meanwhile the dementia of our metaphysics, popular and professional, spreads unchecked. Mind and its presumed 'states' are internal—*inside* some nonentity not specified. Matter is all *outside* this nonentity.[1] Distinction is all one with division. Roots become generating spores for the purposes of argument, or discharge the functions of ova.

[1] The obvious fact that space is 'internal' precisely as much—or little—as it is 'external' is, strangely enough, ignored. We might as well treat the spatial as 'upward' while using 'downward' for the non-spatial.

A spectre becomes a spirit. The world of experience, and our every thought about it, have
ultimately a 'solid basis,' from which they must
never move on pain of destruction. Light is
dangerous, and must not be thrown upon the
origin or reason of Belief, which is, of course,
the same thing as Faith. What you *have*, from
a house to a skin, a prejudice, and a self, is what
you *are*. Pursue materialism, spiritism, pessimism, and all forms of rigid orthodoxy to their
ultimate end, you will always find the implicitly
false mental image, source of the false linguistic
image. You will always find a remediable
ocular defect in a 'seeing' mind, which is
presumably no more perfect than its physical
analogue the eye, but which is, like that, able to
assist in rectifying the data of touch, smell, and
hearing, and even those rightly or wrongly
resulting from its own activity.

VI

PROFESSOR KARL PEARSON long ago submitted that
in consequence of the fetishistic use of the terms
matter, mass, motion, force, space, time, cause,
atom, body, law, etc. (especially in text-books),
physical science has made a false start. But the
biologist, the physiologist, the psychologist have
all been dependent on such terms, since no
others were current when they adopted their
terminology ; and have taken them perforce in
untenable and misleading senses. In these senses
they have everywhere used them both directly
and figuratively, and have passed them on into
literary and popular usage. Therefore, if Prof.
Pearson's position is capable of being maintained
even in the broadest sense, Psychology and
Ethics have so far made a false start also. It
follows that their premisses are liable to vanish
along with the superannuated connotations of
the main-artery terms of physical science. At
all events, if the modern scientist is compelled to
use the old terms—taking them over as Chemistry

took over the terms of Alchemy, as Astronomy took over the terms of Astrology—due care should be taken to charge them publicly with new meanings, and so bring the popular mind into effective relation with its own vocabulary. Owing to this not having been done, the popular mind to-day is still largely steeped in the logic of magic, and yet seldom suspects it.   And perhaps most where it least suspects it.   For the securest stronghold of myth is just the mind which, in the name of common sense, refuses to question its own certainties.

Let a single example be cited of the way in which the so-called common-sense mind, starting from a misconception of the facts, confidently uses this misconception as the source of analogies and metaphors to which it gives authoritative and directive significance.   Our eyes, as science now tells us, are "focussed to infinity."   It is their nature to look away : the distant vision is more germane to them (and us) than the inspection of things minute or immediately near. Here, surely, is a truth of great illuminating potency.   But the 'common-sense' mind starts from quite a different conception of the facts, and draws a corresponding inference.   It assumes a morbid shortsightedness as normal.   It supposes that the hard thing, the effort, the strain, is to

look far away, to look beyond this or that
'limit': that our eyes are 'formed' to see
with least trouble the things close to us, and
therefore are most properly occupied with these
things.   And so the false premiss gets translated,
by the fatal process of false metaphor, into a
common-sense and unanswerable protest against
every tendency to any kind of "transcendental-
ism" as being futile, a foolish attempt to reverse
the wholesome order which makes the near
world within touch or grasp our business, fits
the mind for that, and condemns us to stretch
and strain painfully if we would look towards
what is beyond our reach ;—*that is, our arm-
stretch.*

Here, then, we have an instance of how the
use of analogy and metaphor derived from a false
view of the facts may result in an effective
arrest or more mischievous misdirection of
thought, and so in a further and deeper obscuration
of truth.

A reference to the function of the rods and
cones, as the receivers of light, would afford
another instructive instance of useful analogy
excluded and lost to us by the persistence of
phrases which perpetuate the effects of earlier
ignorance.   But, indeed, the same testimony and
lesson occurs throughout all our thinking.   We

are always appealing to facts to furnish us with illustrations, and we are right in doing so. But if our appeal is really to a mere fancy which we are treating as a fact; if we seriously take the centaur as we take the 'horse' and the 'man,' and use its supposed movements as the analogues of something we want to illustrate, arguing from the one to the other as though a 'man-horse' were a 'fact' in 'nature'; then, of course, we re-import into our reasoning, by a misuse of expression, the very errors and fallacies which reason is chiefly occupied in exposing and removing.

If we appeal to a centaur at all, it must be as a fabulous monstrosity used to illustrate something else monstrous. But we too often use 'facts' of the centaur, or satyr, or dragon, or phœnix class, whereby to express the reasonable, the congruous, the orderly, the real; for instance, matter, force, spirit, cause, etc. in their popular or inherited sense. They create difficulties which else would not exist.

VII

WE always tend unconsciously to make whatever we have expressed in images and through metaphor behave like the 'real thing' or the original which we took as illustration or in analogy. Hence results endless confusion, the real source of which is not detected, and is therefore permitted to continue its mischievous work.

Take our use of Inner and Outer as metaphorical expressions of the mental and physical. Through the influence of that usage we instinctively try to make our minds, our ideas and thoughts, behave as if they were shut up inside definite bounds, that is, as if they were objects in space. Hence a false psychology, and educational ideals and methods that aim at the development—or production—of thinking machines, from which you grind out any desired product, coupled with a thought-cabinet with innumerable drawers, a thought-cupboard with innumerable shelves and cavities.

But sometimes this tendency is overcome in some related metaphor, which has to be forced into harmony with the falsity thus produced. *E.g.* we speak of introspection, of looking into our own consciousness, etc.   The mental eye which looks inward is so far assumed, for the purposes of the occasion, to be 'outer' despite of its being mental and so (*ex hypothesi*) 'inner.' But biology knows of no visual organs which introspect, which turn on an axis or are fixed, to look 'inwards.'   We are *not* intended to inspect our own 'internal economy' in action.

But having settled that the mental world exists inside some kind of containing outline, we have to invent impossible mental eyes that look inward before we can use the 'introspective method.'   No wonder science protests against that method, though she does not seem to realise the initial reason for such protest.

Take again the Basis and Foundation.   We try to consider things which are really—like the world itself—quite independent of a 'firm base,' as 'founded securely' upon this and that.   But all 'foundation' on which we build has no security for itself save a deeper layer under it, and beyond that—nothing, or the ether.

VIII

AMONG the many defeating absurdities of current imagery perhaps that of ' laws of nature ' is one of the worst.   One would really think sometimes that nature had primordially summoned councils and decreed laws, or even brought in a bill in some Natural Assembly, discussed it, passed it, clause by clause, carefully defining its regulations and penalties !   And one would think that nature's lawyers and judges expounded or laid down her laws and enforced her decrees, imposing the statutory penalties for their infringement.   For, of course, we are supposed to ' break ' nature's ' laws '—though the idea is as grotesque as it would be to suppose that we can break the ' law ' of identity and difference, or the ' law ' that $2 + 2 = 4$.

It may be said, and is constantly said in similar cases, that the image being a mere convenience, no one is misled by it.   That is surely in all cases a profound error.   True that

we are not consciously misled.   But our 'sub-
sequent proceedings' — our whole system of
references to man's relation to nature, to the
ethical import of reality in the widest sense—
betray the fact that we are all the more
dangerously misled because we have no suspicion
of being so.   Witness the much-confused and
morbid optimism and pessimism which is the
final outcome of our supposed observing, keeping,
or breaking of nature's "laws."   What to one
of us seems a faultless legislative system, one
by means of which discovery and exploitation
of the universe by man becomes possible, to
another seems a system of 'inhuman' tyranny
and ruthless coercion, involving cruel and senseless waste of power, and outrage upon life.   One
man flies in despair to the ' supernatural,'
while another sets his teeth and tries to con-
vince himself that he lives under an absolute
government of what he calls ' mechanical
forces'; subject like the 'material' to immut-
able laws from which there is no escape, since
an automatic policeman stands, or a patent lock
is fixed, at every gate by which he might pass
out into freedom and the larger, better, and
more justly-ordered life which he has ideally
conceived.

IX

A FEW examples may here be noted of a kind of metaphorical usage which oftener tends to throw dust in our eyes than to throw light on any subject, starting as it does from veiled fallacy or false assumption, now discredited by growing experience or widening and increasingly exact knowledge.

As we have already seen, the use of Internal and External, Inner and Outer, Within and Without, Inside and Outside, as means of contrasting mind and body, consciousness and nature, psychical and physical, thought and reality, is radically misleading. So also is the use of basis and foundation to express a primary or ultimate need; and, in lesser degree, the use of ground and root for the same purpose. The first introduces in all sorts of connections the fallacies of primitive cosmogony. 'Ground' is only needed for standing, walking, dancing upon; for planting in or building or mining, very rarely for grasping or holding. Roots, again,

26

only belong to a plant stage of existence, and are
sent down to obtain nourishment and give a grip,
or hold, for the plant.   Yet all these are used
indiscriminately as though they covered or illus-
trated the whole range of accessible realities and
characteristic experiences of Man.   There is, in
fact, the whole scheme of material, substantial,
static analogy and metaphor for the psychical or
mental or intellectual (or 'spiritual') sphere.

There are, again, the metaphors — rather,
perhaps, the figurative phrases—which depend
on 'absolute' criterions of time, space, etc. ; or
on an 'absolute' cosmical centre, and on 'im-
passable' gulfs which split up the whole fabric
of experience and the inclusive sum of knowledge
into isolated fragments, and thus bring into
existence 'insoluble enigmas' ; these last mostly,
it may be, dependent on the prevalent confusion
between *distinction and division or separation.*

There are the misused metaphors of sense ;
beginning with 'grasp' or 'touch' and 'tangible,'
and ending with 'speculation,' the 'visionary,'
'insight,' a 'clear outlook,' a 'comprehensive
view,' etc. ; these, again, all used indiscriminately as covering the whole field of experience,
and of equal illustrative value in every connec-
tion.   In all these cases the effect of the attempt
to give to strictly limited or specific images an

almost universal prevalence and application is, that their real value in use — the value which they might yield in intellectual use—is largely forfeited, and we are not even aware of the loss.

Finally, there is the imagery which gives peculiar sanction and almost sacredness to the straight line produced to infinity, though no one has ever seen it there.   But of the tolerated inanities of superseded analogy there is indeed no limit.

X

WE all "compound for sins we are inclined to,
By damning those we have no mind to." Thus
we are now freely banning as 'superstition' the
animistic and mythical beliefs of our forefathers
regarding the nature of things. Yet all the
while we retain these very associations in our
inherited language, the surface-sense only being
altered, and the old associations being unconsciously but coercively called up in the
'subconscious' region whence come the most
powerful of our impulses and tendencies, since
there acts not merely the individual but the Race
whose tradition he carries.

At any rate our ancestors did not do that.
Their expressions called up the associations then
valid, and their metaphors entirely harmonised
with their supposed realities and facts. The
difference between then and now is that our
metaphors are divorced from our facts ; and
this often involves worse confusion than the

wildest fetishism, or when it does not, defeats us by excluding that appeal to association which is the very optic nerve of thought as reflecting reality.

XI

WHAT a new mental world we should enter if
we learned to pause in the act of using imagery,
and to scrutinise intelligently our own and our
' opponent's ' figurative habits ! What dis-
coveries we should make as to why some true
and fruitful thought is so unwillingly received
or is even rejected with protest by those to
whom we should have expected it especially to
appeal ! We refer these effects now to ' cussedness ' in things or in human nature ; but then
we should perceive that the initial ' cussedness '
is rather in our barbaric speech than in the
mind to which it gives such distorted expression.
Then would come an era in which, instead of
begging our reader not to take our imagery
seriously, not to apply its implications, but to
regard them as incidental excrescences of conventional expression, we should rather bid him,
in certain cases, to lay these implications to
heart for all they were worth or could
yield.

We could safely afford to do so ; for then we should select the imagery which is to convey our meaning with the same scrupulous discrimination which the jeweller, the surgeon, or the electrician uses in selecting the implements for the finest processes of his work.   Our analogies then would not only ' hold water '— pure water from the well of truth—but they would ' stand fire '—the hottest fire of criticism or the crucible of test.   They would *work* in all senses ; not only as being consistently applicable, but as rendering profitable service ; indicating rich harvests, pointing the way to fresh lines of inquiry and modes of interpretation.   The more they were analysed the more they would suggest and convey as their implications came into view.

True that the reality and the image can seldom if ever entirely coincide, that the most felicitous illustration stops short somewhere and fails to ' cover the whole ground.'   But if the indirect mode of expression, so often the only one available for conveying the most precious and vital truths of life, were gradually assimilated to a world of order instead of remaining a tolerated chaos, we should all be taught betimes to recognise the limits of comparison or parallel. When in doubt, we should ask whether this or that inference really ' presses an analogy too far,' and whether some other analogy, equally apt, would bear ' pressing ' farther, and so bring us a step nearer to the truth.

XII

To give one out of the mass of illustrations needed : Suppose a man engaged in controversy says, " I take my stand upon that fact." Three questions may arise.

(1) Does he mean what he says ? That is, does he really intend to convey the image which the words express ? If so, we might go on to ask, how *does* one " take one's stand upon " a fact ? Is one found invariably trampling it, or is it always under one's heel ? Does one never move with regard to it, so as to look at it or use it, especially in an argument ?

(2) Is he telling us the actual truth, or is it on some other fact, unavowed or unrecognised, that he is really " taking his stand " ?

(3) Is he figurating accurately, that is, appropriately and thus helpfully ?

The last question is hardly ever asked, and yet it is the key to the other two.

For suppose that another man in the same controversy ' takes his stand ' upon another 'fact.' Then in any case if the figure is accurate—that is, appropriate—they can never meet or even approximate, and to the argument there will be no end.

But if the first man says, "I take my departure from that point," or "I start on that line," and the second replies, "And I from (or on) this other"—then the possibility of deflection at least comes in, to help them to a solution or agreement.   For alter direction in either case, and the lines may sooner or later meet at one point, perhaps at several ; or the two may even run for a little way together.   Then they may once more diverge—or they may cross.

Now, will any one deny that the latter is a better image than the former for what we require in discussion ? that is, a more helpful type of image for mental process, incident, and purpose ?

Generalising, we may say : Grant but the idea of motion—the minimum intellectual postulate in a moving world—and there is always the hope, and almost the certainty, of the most widely divergent 'views' or ways of putting it consistent with reason and fact meeting somewhen, somewhere.   And meanwhile their 'holders' may have traversed a whole universe of assimilable experience.   Not, we will hope, as a rolling stone gathering no moss, but as the little creature which gathers silica as it creeps, to form an exquisite shell-home.   Or, better still, as the amœba ingests and transforms food, new substance for its own vital growth, acquired by sensitive contact with the nutritive reality around it.

XIII

Upon the whole, therefore, it may be truly said
that imagery, as we are content to use it, is liable
to be insane in two senses : in the sense of
raving, and in the sense of *waste*. In the first
place, it is as though we were shouting at random
and talking nonsense ; in the second, as though
we were throwing food out of the window
and money into the sea. The two combined
represent sheer and cruel loss and paralysis of
thought.

Paralysis of thought. For do what we will,
we cannot escape the law which unites, as in our
very eye, image and object, reflection and reality,
— sign and what it signifies, figure and the figurate,
and, generally, token or symbol and what they
stand for. Those of us who consciously think
pictorially are so far more or less able to realise
the gravity and extent of this insidious danger.
But those of us who do not are in far worse
case. They do not even receive automatic
warning of the mischief going on. And the

difficulties which their thinking presently en-
counters are of course traced to the wrong
source — probably charged to Nature or to
human ignorance, or to the innate perversity of
original principles. But it is needless to defend
Nature, which presents problems, as it were, in
order that we may learn how simply they may
be solved ; while as to original principles, we
may complain of their innate perversity when
we have begun to agree as to what they are.
And as to human ignorance, that is scarcely a
valid excuse, so long as we do our best to preserve such ignorance, both by the tolerated mis-
fits of imagery in actual use, and by the neglect
to provide for a constantly growing adequacy
of language : not merely through accretion of
new words, but also through the drastic critique
of imagery and the resulting acquirement of
more fitting idioms, figures, and expressive forms
in general.

It is part of the same costly folly to allow,
as we do, such daily additions in slang and
popular talk as tend to create fresh confusion.
And this is the more reprehensible, because both
slang and popular talk, if intelligently regarded
and appraised, are reservoirs from which valuable
new currents might be drawn into the main
stream of language—rather perhaps armouries

from which its existing powers could be continuously re-equipped and reinforced.

The poet very largely shares with the scientist the responsibility of maintaining and worsening the evil tradition of unsound and therefore insane imagery. For instance, when Mr. William Watson writes of "foundations in the world's heart," he deserves to undergo such a world's experience and to have figurative foundations in his own figurative heart! For foundations—we must hope of solid and immovable stone, or preferably of impermeable concrete—in a physical heart would be more fatal even than ossification. In truth, Nature seems to have taken a deserved vengeance, and left us to the solid stone basis or foundation on which we are always, out of place, insisting; left us to talk portentously of Life, while in the same breath we explain that it is 'built up' (from our fixed foundations)! and therefore must be a mere aggregate of cemented bricks or stones with no nexus but cement.

Considering all these things, the question suggests itself, Can we be fully alive yet? Have we even a glimmering of the Sense of which we talk so vaguely and confusingly? Do we so much as suspect what such a Sense as ours ought to be, and do, and preserve us from ?   Do we ever dream of the almost Utopian results which must accrue when the sense of our symbols becomes really fitting ; when we find really good sense and common sense, and are sensitive in the best sense, in our estimate and treatment of the cardinal questions of that expression on which alike depend practical activities and the thinking which alone controls, directs, interprets, applies, and utilises them ?

There is need of some great poet to write worthily, from a fresh view-point, on the Power of the Word—the word which we blow about as though it were but chaff, gravely explaining indeed that it is 'merely word,' and so implicitly of no moment.   But our use of words is never that ; for whether positive or negative, excessive or deficient, present or absent even, our words are of moment always.   "For the first time," says a recent writer, "there swept over him that awful sense of unavailing repentance for the word said which might so well have been left unsaid, which most human beings are fated to feel at some time of their lives."   Aye ; but the author should have included the *word unsaid*, which has often helped or hindered, and in all human ways signified so much.   Indeed, that word 'merely' is constantly misused and per-

haps never more so than in conjunction with
'verbal.'   Let us tread softly with our merelys,
onlys, simplys . . . and use them with fear
and trembling.   Yet even in silence there is no
escape for us either from danger or duty.   Silence
is often a most significant declaration, and a most
misleading one.

There is but one safety ; and that is, to realise
as we have never done yet what we are doing
with speech, and what with significant silence.
And we have to realise vitally, intimately,
actively, the power of symbol not only in
Word, as in legend, narrative, parable, name,
and all social speech and all intellectual discus-
sions ; but also in act, as in ritual, ceremony,
performance, posture, dance.   There has been
as yet no adequate, no thorough, no logical and
scientific attempt on the widest basis to deal
with this central interest of man's expression and
realisation of himself and the world through
Symbol ; no attempt, with this paramount object
in view, to wed the sacred and the secular, the
emotional and the intellectual domains and
examples.   But indeed it cannot be adequately
done until we know what the Word really is ;
until at long last we begin worthily to speak ;
until we understand that the Word may be, as
in our usage it often is, a mere articulate sound

with a mean sense, a capricious, idle, abusive meaning,—or, as also a Child, a Son, a Divine Messenger, and Reason itself are bearers and expressions of the Significance of life.

XIV

CAN we even appraise the value of the Symbol ?
Can we, say by any effort of imagination, place
ourselves at the standpoint of the unfortunate in
the limbo of the Asymbolic, hungering and
yearning for the Sign that gives significance,
albeit with no likeness to itself, yet giving us the
world of the indicated and implied ; signalling
the messages which are there to be interpreted
and to be acted upon as rousing, drawing, re-
assuring, or warning us ?

We know something of the thirst of the
excluded when, loving the holy, we know
ourselves unholy ; when, looking up with intellectual reverence to knowledge and the will
and power to wield it — to the creative or
victorious energy of the leader, the man we
call great—we know ourselves ignorant, supine,
indifferent in comparison ; stupid or silly, superficial, or (as we say of the hardminded) commonplace and unresponsive.

Well, at least it is something to know ourselves

all that and worse. For *who* is thus confessing
and lamenting ?   That is a divine discontent.
But sharper than all the pangs of such perception,
sadder even than such sense of humiliation and
banishment, would be the pangs of the prisoner
of the asymbolic limbo looking up with infinite
longing and yearning at the treasures we so
amazingly disregard, or abuse and despise.

All other powers have come under the higher
brain of Man ; that wonderful enabling instrument of orderly creation which does for mind
what so-called Law, conceived of as a marshalling
and directive principle in the physical world,
may be pictured as doing for motion and matter.
But the real power of symbol in its articulate
and logical form ; the real function of the word
in this sense ; the power of sense itself, of meaning itself, and of that significance which is pre-
eminently the glory of speech : this power is as
yet practically in abeyance and almost pitiably
ignored.   For we are all guilty of or tolerate in
this matter a dereliction, an ignoration and a
waste which we should not suffer to continue
for a day in any other case of vital importance
or even of interested curiosity.

XV

IT might be useful (and there may be more
warrant for it than we know) if we were to
regard the physical world as a complex acted
metaphor of the mental world, and both as
essentially expressive of a common nature.

Be it premised that 'language' is a term
which admits of being used in a wide sense, as
poets and philologists both know and teach us.
May it be, then, that as our eyes reverse the
position of external objects and the brain has to
restore it : as our consciousness gives as at least
world-wide, the field of view which is in reality
no larger than the eye itself : so in fact does
Nature speak to us in a language of unerringly
fitting metaphor and valid analogy, by simply
doing what 'she' does : manifesting her doings
gradually to our growing intelligence through
what we call 'sense,' but keeping a margin of
reserve in her yet undiscovered or unrelated
secrets ? May it be that our 'speech' is but
an awkward, half-adjusted, and therefore confused

and ambiguous rendering or re-presentation of the irrefutable eloquence of natural phenomena ?

We look to the material for metaphors of the mental ; we trace up most words and phrases—perhaps all—to the physical. But we are also constrained to reverse this process : we find *e.g.* that emotional terms best picture and help us to realise some qualities in physical nature.   And in fact does not the physical world require the mental world as that whereby to represent itself, as we know that the red rose requires the light for its redness, while in its turn the light is only completed or rendered operative by that responsive activity we call ' sight ' ? Supposing that we personified Nature in a scientific sense, postulating her as a unified series of impressions, would she now be found speaking of us in a metaphor as we of her, only with speech reversed ?   That is, would her every ' word ' be taken metaphorically from the action or process of consciousness, reason, reflection, judgment ?   Thus might we not say that motion, and mass, and the so-called ' matter ' assumed as behind them, are as full of mind-metaphor as mind is of matter-metaphor ; the mind-metaphor arising in the conscious world, and reaching us through intelligence, and intellect, as matter-metaphor arises in the unconscious world, and reaches us through sense ?

XVI

WHETHER we see it under that aspect or
another, the fact remains that not only Nature
in the ordinary sense of the term, but also these
human constructions which consist in adaptation
of Nature's properties and material to the use
and service of man, are all charged with potential metaphor of the highest illustrative value.
For the sake of an instance, let us consider the
familiar allegorical way of speaking of human
life as a voyage.

We speak of steering our way or navigating
our course in the "voyage of life." With this
we contrast the rudderless drifting which ends
in wreck, or at least reaches no harbour, and
lands in no port or goal at all, the sailors on
the awful deeps of life. We image in our
minds the sudden hurricane, the impenetrable
fog, the persistent gale, the heavy seas, which
are to try the soundness of our life-ship's
timbers, the training and seamanship of her
officers and crew, and her general seaworthiness.

We recognise the need, not only of efficiency, but of knowledge—and that not merely terrestrial, but cosmical—if we would attain, with the least possible delay or danger, the haven at which we would arrive.   And last, we picture to ourselves the rugged coasts, the sunken rocks, the hidden reefs, the entangling weeds of the shallow waters to which the track of most of us is confined, and which in any case confront us in more or less threatening forms at both ends of our voyage, as well as at intermediate calling-places.

And now, let us ask those who are our beacon-givers in the world of earth and water for such facts as may afford, at least, not false or merely fanciful, but true-to-nature illustrations of what the beacon-givers of mind and conscience ought to bring us for help in our life-voyage.

Here are some answers received from one source out of many, *A Chapter on Lighthouse Work*, by the late Professor Tyndall.[1]   In the first place, let us note that

The atmosphere through which the rays have to pass from the lighthouse to the mariner is the truest photometer.   The opacity of the atmosphere is entirely due to suspended matter, foreign to pure air. . . . Atmospheric opacity is not due to

---

[1] It must not be supposed that an instance like this one is exceptionally valuable.   The wealth of illustrative material that really illustrates and yet is never utilised is little suspected.

absorption, but to the waste of the light *in echoes* from the particles on which the light-waves impinge.

And surely it is equally true that the prevailing ' opacity ' (or denseness) of mind which often usurps the honourable name of ' common-sense '— or the 'practical,' the 'active,' the ' productive ' — is due to " suspended matter foreign to the pure air" of clear, transparent thinking : to 'thoughts' that have really never been thought, but only borrowed by those who hold them.   And this, too, is not due to 'absorption,' which may, so to speak, store up that energy which again may take the form of heat or even light, but to the waste of intellectual and moral force in echoes (or reflex beams) even from a reflective mind or sensitive conscience, when encumbered with much dusty detail, orderless or crowded.

Secondly, let us observe the gain in power (for beacon-work) from the depth of a light-giving flame.

It is depth alone that confers upon the flame its augmented intensity when used in a revolving apparatus.   In this case eight luminous strata send their light simultaneously in the same direction to the lens, the hinder strata radiating *through* the layers of flame in front of them.

So, even when we do find minds which give out light, how thin, and thus how weak to penetrate, it mostly is !   How true we feel the

E

principle to be, that if revealing power is to come, and mariners be safely guided on their way, there must be layers of flame of which the inner ones shall radiate through the outer. And even that is not the only need ; for 'lateral divergence' must be given to the rays, else much will still remain in outside shadow, of which we need a warning right and left. But all we yet have reached by our means of mental aid and guidance falls short of 'group-flashing.'

In the material beacon this "gives the impression that there is life in it"; that it is "actively exerting itself to warn" and guide. And what, after all, is life ? Has it not been said to be, in some sense, "latent in a fiery cloud"? Why may it not have affinity of some kind (through consciousness) with light ?[1] To quote again :

A point connected with physiological optics deserves mention here. The optic nerve is partially and rapidly paralysed by light ; and the value of the group-flashing light is enhanced by the fact that during the intervals of darkness the eye in great part recovers its sensibility and is rendered more appreciative of the succeeding shock. The suddenness of the illumination and the preparedness of the retina are points to which I always attached importance. The thrilling of distant lightning through dense clouds suggests an idea to be aimed at in

---

[1] Since this was written, electricity has brought life and light into very close relation.

experiments of this character. . . . The more I think of it,
and the more I experiment upon it, the more important does
this question of flashes appear to me. . . . It is its suddenness
that renders the lightning flash so startlingly vivid through a
cloud. . . .

Too seldom do we try to translate facts like
these into the dialect of mind-vision.. The
sight-nerves of our mind get numbed and dulled
by that continuous light impression which we
ignorantly treasure.   An interval of darkness we
abhor ; a time of shadow is to us a horror.   We
even strive to nullify its service, insisting on
persistent, unbroken light from whatever source,
of whatever quality, without one respite to the
tired mind-eyes ; and then we shake our heads
and cry, "We cannot see ; at least there is
nothing visible, we are sure of that."   And yet
the pause may be the means of better seeing—
may be the actual secret of the keenest sight
we have.   The law of rhythm claims obedience
thus ; each self and all the race must say, Amen.
And let us bear in mind that 'laws' like this
act through vast ages of development.   A week
or even a thousand years of darkness may mean,
to race or unit, one vibration.   What matter, if
to rested eyes light flashes, coming when they
can use it to good purpose, revealing, making
clear, the ways of life ?

XVII

THERE are few things more unintelligent, because wasteful where economy is especially needed, than our use of certain popular metaphors. This is one of the many cases in which present education, as it were, permits notorious and re-movable obstacles to block the path of mental advance, or connives at the true lines of that advance being constantly warped. The result is something fairly equivalent on the mental plane to mis-pronunciation and mis-spelling on the social one.

We rightly correct with care these last tendencies, not merely as a matter of custom, but also because neither ignorance nor neglect of rule, nor peculiarities of dialect, however racy in their effect, must be allowed to complicate the unanimity and ease of intercourse. Having corrected slipshod usage in matters of sound and form, we proceed to grammar, and replace caprice or disorder by consistency and order; explaining always that not merely custom but economy and expressiveness are at stake.   Finally, we add some training in at least elementary logic, sufficient for the conduct of social life and thinking at various given levels of requirement or use.

One may venture, indeed, to think that some of these precautions are too rigidly taken ; that expressiveness, apt, fitting, pungent, illuminative, illustrative, suggestive, is often needlessly sacrificed by our hastily denouncing instead of adopting some apt and significant idiom or accent or spelling of unsophisticated dialects, or of the child's spontaneous speech.   But then, if we did in that direction seek to enrich, economise, and invigorate language, we should have to be careful in so doing to make it less cumbersome, less wordy, less pedantically formulative than popular speech frequently is.   We must see that our contributions neither impoverish nor sacrifice quality in accumulating a larger choice ; that they lessen neither dignity, grace, nor delicacy. Even the whimsical, when admitted, must be obviously subservient to the one great need and rule : concentrated, apt, effective, and terse expressiveness.   When usage has been made as flawless as we can make it, beauty must inevitably follow.   But the instrument must be 'in perfect tune' before the musician can entrance us or even attract us by his playing.

Now, in this sphere of imagery, analogy, metaphor, trope, etc.— in short, of linguistic comparison, reflection, parallel, or likeness—we find one of the most notable examples of our inconsistency. Whereas we press convention and formality into a rigid 'board-school' or 'academic' mould, and risk loss on this side, we are curiously careless,— generally, indeed, unsuspicious,—of the fact that we are liable to be powerfully swayed by the unintentional suggestions of language ; as when the common or direct use of a word or phrase infects, so to speak, its analogical or metaphorical use.

Our analogical use of the terms solid ground, basis, foundation, has been already dealt with, but is worth considering more closely. Nothing can be more interesting or educative than the racial history of the stress we lay on these physical facts and the mental use we make of them. Nothing can be more admirable than the service they can and often do render. But it is none the less lamentable that for many generations teachers should, instead of leading in the path of rational linguistic advance, have followed fortuitous degenerative usage, and perpetuated actual ignorance of facts, actual confusion of thought, in the use of analogies of this kind. Before the days of Galileo, as it must be remembered and insisted on, the use of solid ground, basis, and foundation, as figures of universal and primary necessity, or of ultimate security, was entirely justified.   The earth itself was assumed to be securely founded ; and its being detached from its basis and set whirling in space was the last thing which there was any reason to fear.   Solid ground was the need of the very world we lived on : to be 'supported on nothing' was crashing ruin.

Well, so it still is for us men.   We must have a firm substratum to stand and yet more to build upon.   To build ? yes : with wood, brick, stone, or concrete, our shelters, defences, huts, towns.   All must be as firmly founded as the tree is rooted.

Yet even now we are making aeroplanes, not merely geoplanes ; and daily inventing fresh means of speeding through air without touch of earth or water.   Therefore, we have less excuse than ever for forgetting the secure and powerful flight of the bird, or the fact that the earth on which we build so heavily rests, or rather floats, more safely on the bosom of space than a soap-bubble on the air.   And when the time comes when some of us shall work and practically live in the air in some roomy air-boat anchored in our garden, and only descend to solid earth for food or other need, we may then, perhaps, recognise practically what science has long ago announced to us, that the ultimate 'foundations' of all visible power are neither builded nor built upon, but are sources of energy and centres of force, the suns and atoms of the cosmos. And recognising this, we shall perhaps permit the fact to have its proper influence, not only on our views of life, but on our ways of expressing that and ourselves.

XVIII

PHRASES like 'the material world,' 'human life,' 'spiritual experience,' 'heavenly aspiration,' 'insoluble problem,' 'matter of fact,' 'measurable and calculable value,' the 'actual' or 'prosaic' reality are bandied about, sometimes with literary skill, sometimes merely as controversial weapons, sometimes as conventions handed down by those who meant to convey by them conceptions or assumptions which are now either obsolete or greatly changed in bearing. Correspondingly, terms like Nature, matter, force, mass, spirit, mind, and much current image, metaphor, and analogy are used in undetected confusion and a welter of defeating inconsistency. Instead of being informed, directed, enlightened by them — which is the purpose that each of them was originally made to serve—we have either to think away their inherited associations, which is really an addition to the labour of thinking, or else to allow our most momentous conclusions to be vitiated by them. What such vitiation costs us is to be seen in the present enormous waste of exposition and controversy as well as in difficulties and deadlocks actually created by the lack of a real consensus in the quest and achievement of an adequate, consistent, ever intensifying and expanding Expression.

If we realised the situation and acted upon it, the results must at first appear miraculous, like recovery of sight by the lifelong blind ; or rather, perhaps, like the exploits of the primitive kindlers of fire and constructors of weapons, tools, boats, wheels, etc., and of grammatical language itself, who were the real leaders of the race.

But for this very reason it is easier at present to take concrete cases, in which the choice is bewilderingly wide, since we are "all in the same boat." From one end to the other in our speech and writing we have the too futile complaint that this or that obsolete convention or current custom compels us here, hinders us there, in ways which ought not to be tolerated for a moment. And the complaining author himself inevitably, though in varying degrees, falls into the trap which he is denouncing.

Undoubtedly we are all in the same boat. For the critic who writes from the point of view

of Significs, that is, from the really expressive,
descriptive and interpretative standpoint, has fre-
quent occasion to remember that he has no other
means of protest and exposition than current
language, the very one which so urgently calls for
them. All that is said or written, therefore, by the
significian, is necessarily itself subject to the very
criticism which he brings and urges. And, meanwhile, the literary expert or the artist in verbal
expression only reveals by his mastery of phrase
or his brilliant use of imagery or comparison,
and by the ease, dignity, and harmonious flow of
his diction, how much more we might hope for
if his powers were really set free, and his readers
trained to welcome what, as working in a purified
and enriched medium, he could give us.

XIX

STORIES used to be told of a man who always explained to his servants that "when I ask for a corkscrew I mean a carving-knife." One knows now that this is quite a common form of memory disease. But we all virtually do this without the warning! We take for granted that the needed shift—the tacit "he does not mean what he says but the other unsaid thing" —is automatically made, as no doubt to some extent it is.

But why, in this world of crowding obstacle to a clear mental path, do we tolerate even the minutest avoidable barrier to the smooth and swift running, in coupled order, of thought and speech? It is just as cheap and easy to use the root image or the foundation image or other like ones in the case where they do fit, and some other image or figure where they don't, as it is to persist in a falsifying usage. Any one who has learnt to notice these things may many a time detect in conversation the sub-attentive

results of leaving our linguistic instrument out
of tune.   What should we say to a violin player
who smiled and said, What does it matter that
my instrument isn't tuned?   You all know what
note I mean to play ; you can all by habit set it
right or ignore it.   And the same excuse avails
for the player of a false note, which may easily
become a convention to people who have
defective 'ears.'   "O, he does not mean F
sharp but F flat !"   Doubtless too many of us
have defective ears in this sense, and both commit
and tolerate much discord without knowing it.
But still, the commonest strummer who wrote or
printed a jingle, and then played it, would be
pulled up by his hearers if he not only used flats
and sharps and other notes indiscriminately, but
justified it by saying, "Nobody is misled !"
These things are all convention, and one note
does as well as another if it is accepted as the
proper thing.

And it is true that these things, in musical
composition or rendering, do little harm beyond
tormenting the sensitive ear.   The practical
world goes on placidly while we play sharp for
flat, and accepts the one for the other.   But the
corresponding state of things in all expression ;
the obscurity and ambiguity of our expressive
score, the use in language of a (perhaps faintly)

discordant note or a half-tuned instrument—even though passably right to an artificially dulled ear —*that* is an unthinkable loss to the interests and the powers of Man, whose ideal, surely, is to be embodied harmony, like the normal organism, and consciously faultless Expression.   Discord in this domain does not merely torture the mental analogue of a musical ear.   It makes for mental confusion and obstruction ; it needlessly adds to difficulties already serious enough, and lessens the too scanty treasure of illuminative thought and communicative power.

Even at the best we can do and think and say too little that is really worth while in the fullest sense.   Our noblest eloquence is confessed by the worker, thinker, poet, to fall short of a true mark.   But we are profoundly stirred ; great and wise and beautiful things are conveyed to us, and we rise in response beyond the self of commonplace with which we have no right to be content.   Only, that response is unconsciously impoverished and even distorted by quite avoidable drawbacks, which we not only complacently tolerate but teach to children, thus ensuring their permanence and stifling the instinct of right expression which, though in quaint forms, shows itself clearly in the normal child until successfully suppressed.   And though

we do now and then recoil from a glaring
misuse of term in the ' rising generation,' and
lament such a lapse from *our* good ways, we
never see that the fatal seed has been sown, the
fatal tradition of a far more extensive misuse has
been handed on, by us ; that in scores and
hundreds of instances we have carefully habitu-
ated the child, trained it, to say one thing when
it means another, or to be content to leave much
of language in rags or else cramped by antique
armour.

And, be it remembered, not language only
suffers by this toleration of what is perverse and
impoverishing. In ' art ' some painters or com-
posers would apparently make up for the lack of
original genius or freshness of idea, by a deliber-
ate reversion to barbarism or by an elaboration
which is merely artificial and sophisticated.
This tendency, in fact, runs through all forms of
expressive activity—and is there any form of
activity non-expressive, be it only of the inanity
of the actor ?

XX

THE characteristic function of man in the long evolutionary ascent which he has accomplished may be described as Translation. In mind that function has had its work to do, but in the body its effects are most obviously apparent. Man has translated wing into arm, paw into hand, snout into nose. His translations of vital function and ensuing translations of structure have indeed been innumerable, inevitable, triumphant. Why? Because they were always ascending adaptations; because they always meant readiness to change, to develop, to be modified, even to atrophy and thus make room, on occasion, for the purposes of a vital ascent. . . .

Man, then, has been organically and typically plastic. But his language, except in secondary senses or for superficial purposes, is still rigid. If he has any intentions in regard to speech, it manifestly does not heed them as the paw and the wing of an earlier day heeded the promptings of the phyletic will and took new form and power. He has never yet been able to secure the control and direction of that very gift which most differentiates him from the 'dumb' world. Meantime, there are societies and congresses, national and international, for ensuring the command and developing the potencies of almost all the social activities ; all except the one which most profoundly affects and should precede them all. There are reforming movements in every direction except in regard to that which is their very condition—the power, namely, of really expressive and significant definition of feelings, thoughts, and purposes.

XXI

WHAT, broadly speaking, is the difference
between the most perfect of modern instruments,
machines, apparatus of any kind, and those
organic instruments out of which they have
been developed, or for which they have been sub-
stituted ? The difference consists, for practice,
in their greater precision and accuracy. But
this greater precision and accuracy is always
understood as not restricting but widening the
efficiency of the instrument. As its exquisite
complexity increases, it becomes increasingly
adaptable ; and it automatically stops or even
changes its action when a knot or gap or other
incident in working occurs. It is even said that
when some unfavourable condition occurs which
necessitates the intervention of intelligence, a
bell is sounded which brings the expert. Little
by little the instrument assimilates, by the will
of its maker, some fraction of his own power
of adjustment and of flexibility in providing for
small changes or of averting dangers. In all

such examples of engine and instrument we have, in fact, a projection of man's own prerogative of adaptation. Every instrument is, broadly speaking, an extension of sense and organic function.

We have still, however, only a constructed machine, invented and manufactured ; with its limitations relatively rigid and narrow, however much they may have in recent years expanded. It is desirable, therefore, to supplement this ideal of precision by relating it again with the admitted evolution of the hand from flipper and paw. This latter evolution excludes the idea of actual manufacture and even of a conscious and rational will. But it implies a form of what may be called Racial or Phyletic Will, that will which, profiting by the very existence of favourable varieties able to rise above and overcome adverse conditions, makes the work of natural selection possible.

Now, let us combine these two ideas. Think of the exquisite delicacy in both cases. Realise the marvellous subtlety of the response of violin, microscope, or spectroscope, and of the even more astonishing instruments which are almost crowding upon us, and then consider the consummate skill of the trained hand, free *because* determined and because loyal to fact and order—and you have some suggestion of what language is not yet, but has to become. Something of it, but not all.   For Language is Thought in audible activity.

XXII

BUT indeed the example which language has to
follow, and its ultimate scope and limitations,
are those of the phenomenal world itself. We
are therein aware, thanks mainly to the work
of science, that there are many processes and
changes going on and things existing round us
which we cannot directly 'sense' or 'feel.'
In some cases, though we cannot see, hear, or feel
directly, we can do so indirectly ; we can invent
instruments which are sensitive to stimuli to
which we are entirely insensitive. This brings
us an immense extension of our range of sense-
perception. Yet on the other hand, unless
we can either re-acquire forms of excitability
which are found in the animal world—and to
some extent still in the uncivilised world or in
pathological forms—or else evolve fresh response-
power on a still ascending organic spiral, we
must in the last resort be hampered by a
narrowness of sense-range which even threatens
to increase.

In both respects, that of acquiring command of an ever more efficient instrument, and that of intensifying the range of natural awareness, the world of phenomena accessible to us cannot so far be said to have translated itself adequately into our world of words,—into Language.   We experience much that we cannot articulately express, and therefore cannot usefully study or record.   And why ?   Because after all language, in the present sense of the word, is comparatively a late acquisition ; and for reasons which can, though dimly, be discerned, the development of articulate expression has lagged behind all other forms of development since its first great advance in what to us are ' classical ' periods.

And yet the fact of this arrested development, if we only could see it objectively, as an historical phenomenon, might well move us to wonder. For throughout history there has been, apparently, a widely felt instinct that somehow articulate reasoning—the highest because the rationally ordered form of response to our environment and of analysis of experience—was our supreme attribute and prerogative.   The Greek Logos is, of course, the most conspicuous instance of this recognition.   But it may be found, I believe, throughout Oriental tradition and, in ruder forms, in most types of barbarous and even

savage myth.   It seems strange that man should
so completely have lost sight of the full value of
that to which apparently he has hitherto, in the
more exalted as well as the most primitive
historic phases of his being, rendered instinctive
homage.   We shall do well in this context to
remember that though in the spiritual sphere
'inspiration' is first attributed to the speaker
and writer, and 'revelation' comes mainly in
speech or writing, yet both forms really apply
to all original conception, and even to all original
'composition,' not to the literary alone.

XXIII

LANGUAGE might in one aspect be called articulate music. And we may be grateful to the so-called stylists, although in their efforts after beauty they sometimes sacrifice instead of transfiguring significance, and always tend to defeat themselves by making significance secondary. For at least their work recognises some analogy between the ordered harmony of music which we call attunement, and the true ideal of language.

And thus we are reminded that as yet language in ordinary use barely rises above the level of noise, and only suggests the perfect natural harmony which ought to be its essential character. The reason for this, however, is not merely that in language we have failed to develop a full control of our 'singing' power, or that we are still content with the rude instruments of ancient days, although this is to a great extent true. We may put it in another way and, as already suggested, may say that in civilised speech we have acquired linguistic instruments of real complexity and implicit power to render subtle forms of harmony, but that it has never occurred to us to tune them together, to attune them. And we may suppose ourselves to have told one who suggested the need of this that the proposal was pedantic, and that to tune an instrument was to restrict its scope, as the ambiguity of tone and conflict of intention which reduces music to noise means a valuable freedom secured.   We are liberating music by ostracising the tuner, enriching the language with grunt, squall, yell, squeal, and excruciating discord !

XXIV

WE may experimentally assume that every process really ascertained in physiology fits, has its
corresponding process, in psychology. The
danger is that we are not yet advanced enough
to apply safely the translations in detail which
this natural correspondence should make possible
and instructive ; and a mistranslation would be
worse than none. But if the systematic correspondence be postulated, it should follow that
the advance of knowledge in each sphere ought
to contribute towards advance in the other. The
intrinsic unity is perfect ; witness the existence
of psycho-physics, and even the fact that already
language is full of expressions borrowed from
both sides, though usually in the wrong way
and conveying the wrong idea. Its assumptions being out of date, too much of it is like
talking of railways and steamer traffic in terms
of horse or bicycle traffic ; even as presently we
may be talking of the mis-named ' aviation ' in

terms of tramping and rolling.   This is hardly a caricature.

To some extent, of course, language should carry on the many traditions of experience. But a language loaded with dead traditions has its nerve-channels choked and its reflexes dislocated, and the ensuing general paralysis results in a diseased exuberance of expression.   Of the typical expressive diseases, no adequate diagnosis or even description has yet been made.   Most generally they are of a diffuse, non-acute, negative kind, analogues of a low or deficient vitality.   Healthy action, sound development from simple to complex, and thus to a higher level of simplicity and economy, is usually suppressed in children by their teachers ; so are spontaneous and needed returns to an early heritage of pregnantly significant idiom.   What English has lost in this way can only be guessed at.   The epigrams of folk-speech which linguistic folk-lore collects and preserves afford examples, and so do the few early narratives we have.   But much can never have been committed to writing, or been noticed even to be ridiculed !

Meanwhile, to return to our analogy, linguistic disease in various forms is assiduously imparted or at best left untreated.   We helplessly accept our general paralysis, our dropsy, our cancer of speech ; and the many forms of mental indigestion which result from indulgence in unwholesome speech-food are but one type of the mental ills caused by, and causing, the expressional ills. For the mischief is, of course, reciprocal.

In one case—that alone called ' bad language ' —we do realise this ; we do understood the powerful reaction on mind and character which forms of speech may involve. But unhappily bad language, in a wider sense, is imposed upon our writers and thinkers from the first, and convention chains them to it.

XXV

THERE can be, of course, no question of the convenience and economy of using one word in many senses. The ever-increasing richness and variety of experience would else make vocabularies impossibly cumbrous. The wealth of variation in language, far from being an evil, is a priceless advantage. Outside the region of technical notation, mechanical precision of outline or constancy of content would be both the cause and sign of arrested growth or decaying life. What is wanted is to secure that each of us shall know better where others are, and he himself is, in the matter of expression ; also that we shall allow more than we do yet for the general failure to classify and appraise the shifting penumbras which surround the symbols of thought. We are too apt to assume the true analogy of language to be a world without atmosphere in which every outline is clear cut and sharp ; whereas a truer analogy is that of the world enveloped in an atmosphere which

causes outlines to melt and vary, to shift and
disappear, to be magnified, contracted, distorted,
veiled, in a thousand changing conditions.   These
changes are not drawbacks or dangers except in
so far as they deceive or baffle ; they are the
reflections of life itself as well as of its home.
And in proportion as we are worthy of the
human name in its highest sense, we are able to
understand the significance of, to allow for, even
to exploit that element of uncertainty, of possible
deception, which thus acts as a powerful stimulant
of the higher cerebral activities.   The normal
result of such a stimulation both on the physical
and mental planes is that we learn to interpret,
and to see order and consistency behind, what
have seemed the vagaries of natural hazard.

An assured command of language—one as yet
not even fully possessed by our greatest writers
so long as the immense majority of their readers
have been brought up to misread them or to
read them in incompatible senses—would corre-
spond to that command of mechanical resource
which is the amazing result of the renascence of
the significal function in that one direction.

XXVI

A NECESSARY distinction which is continually
ignored is that between verbal and sensal.[1] The
verbal is question of symbolic instrument regarded
as a thing detached and out of actual use; the
sensal is question of value conveyed thereby on
any particular occasion. The two are at present
hopelessly confused. But no word in actual use
is merely verbal : there and then it is sensal also.
You may have endless variety in the subtle little
tunes or 'airs' that we call words or word-
groups, and in the written symbols which again
stand for these ; but this endless verbal variety
ought to give us an endless sensal treasure. The
sense and meaning, the import and significance
which language carries or makes possible,
constitute its value. What we call its beauty,
partly a verbal and partly a sensal effect, is,
as already suggested, akin to that of music,
which is much more significant than most of

[1] If this word be rejected, we shall require another : but it
conveys a needed variant from sensible.

79

us suppose.   Harmony and melody ought to convey much more to us than they do.

But the idea of *conveyance* is essentially that of the biological tradition and transference which made ascent possible.   Some developments of sense which we had on the animal and doubtless on the primitively human plane have been lost through relaxation of the stress of vital need. Yet in the interests of new mental need we must even try to regain some of these, while acquiring fresh ranges of all senses and fresh subtlety of application.   And with this must go, as part of the same enhancing and vivifying process, fresh delicacy and force of reasoning and fresh intolerance of the confusion in language at present unheeded.

XXVII

IT seems obvious that mathematics should not only become the general benefactor as thus 'applied' to all practical wants, but that it should be equally translatable into other and higher spheres of our common need. But it cannot do this while language (and especially while imagery) remains the neglected discord that it is, even in hands from which one would expect results which throughout rang as true as the music drawn from a perfectly adjusted instrument, and above all from the healthy and most highly organised human larynx. So far from leading to or making for pedantry, this vital command of a perfectly flexible expression in word as in act would reflect the plastic powers of the life-impulse itself in all the richness of its adaptive variation, and would continually surprise us with fresh forms of truth, wonder and beauty, in their turn involving, and in a sense creating, new developments of expressive achievement. At present we see the promise of this gift almost alone on the emotional and imaginative side. The poet does on his own ground surmount the difficulties of language, and by a sort of miracle arouses in us responses which, if we dispassionately analysed his method, we should see to be due to an induced thrill of sympathetic vibration that must ignore the obstacle and exploit emotionally the utmost power of a yet unworthy medium of expression.

But as things are we agree to discount his message, which indeed fails to reach many at all, or to touch, with any perfect healing, the deepest ills, or answer the pregnant questions of life. It is but too evident, also, that the message of religion as yet tends rather to accentuate inevitable differences than to interpret and gather up these into an organic richness of response. Religion, like poetry, comes, as it were, as an isolated lung or an isolated heart, and language is largely to blame for the persistence of this dividing tendency which so effectually breaks up the normal unity of a sane human wholeness on its highest levels.

XXVIII

"LANGUAGE in its present sense," I have said.
For be it confessed at once that I would transcend
the level and limits of mere 'language.' A
mere tongue does not satisfy me except as a
necessary compromise—a detail. What we now
call language is but one, the most comprehensive and delicate, mode of expressing ourselves,
of feeling and thinking together, of articulating
our nature, our knowledge, our hopes, our ideals.
All I care for is first and always that Significance which is reached through sense and meaning, and which (if you give these free play) must
ultimately involve and induce beauty of sound
and form. I am quite ready for the most drastic
changes as well as for the most scrupulous and
anxious preservation of our existing resources all
over the world. I want Greek ; I want Chaucer ;
I want Esperanto, or rather its worthier successor
when that shall appear. I want the Zulu clicks ;
I want modes of expression as yet unused, though
we must not say undreamt of, since there are

many scientist's and idealist's diagrams, symbols
and other 'thinking machines,' all ready and in
order, to rebuke us.

It may be true that the larynx and tongue
must remain the main means. Still, you have
refinement of gesture and of expressive action,
the potentialities of which are practically un-
explored ; and you have the whole field of
'written' symbol and of 'Morse alphabet,' of
the artist's tools and the laboratory apparatus,
open to you. Let us learn to think in radiations
and in ether waves. Let us transfigure grammar
and prosody. Already the poets give us hints of
the plasticity and beauty and wonder of words.
We analyse, yet we do not touch the secret ; but
why not catch at least some of the infection ?
And let us learn to use machinery in higher ways :
let us annex it to the service of thought, of beauty,
of significance. Let us indeed fearlessly accrete
words and phrases from all forms of science. All
the ancient philosophers whom we revere ab-
sorbed the scientific terminology of their day and
used it seriously and exactly. Still more should
we now do this, when science is giving us not
only rudder and compass, but such turbines of
mind as the world has never seen. Nay, is not
acceleration itself just *quickening*, and the whole
of contemporary mechanical development one

parable ?   Language must be regenerated.   It must be re-conceived and re-born, and must grow to a glorious stature.   Of what that may be and become if only we resolve that it shall be, the greatest words of the greatest thinkers give us but a hint.   It is quite ready to serve us : it is only we who are too stupid and vulgar to be worthy of such waiting-on.   We think in the pigmental, and get our 'colour' through mud. Let us think in the spectral, and get our 'colour' through the rainbow.   The true Word, let us realise, is not merely a conventional noise or scrawl or stamp ; it is the Logos, it is Reason. It is more than that.   It is that which can truly say 'I am' : it is the revelation of the Way through truth to life.

XXIX

THE social phenomena of language, observes
M. A. Dauzat,[1] are extremely complex. First
synthesis and then analysis defy the inquirer
(" est rebelle au chercheur "). But this ought
to be the case no more, as no less, than in any
other kind of research which involves the social
conditions of life. It all depends on how we
tackle the problem. If in any subject of human
study we may accept disorder and caprice as our
masters, calling those enslaving factors the inevitable concomitants of ' freedom of will ' and
of an innate tendency to error, of course the
writer's complaint holds good. But it is time
we ceased to make use of the false contrast
between the invariable as mechanical and the
chaotic as voluntary. The will in sound health
has all the trustworthiness of the natural order
and constructed machine, lacking only its indis-
criminative pressure and its senseless persistence
which, dynamically uncontrolled and statically
obstructive, makes for ruin.

[1] *La Vie du langage*, p. 11.

The truly sane mind never errs, never swerves from natural loyalty to the real. It must seek knowledge and ensue it, else it can have no worthy peace. But there is a misunderstood 'ignorance' which really means the attainment of a temporary frontier ; a pause merely to enable us to organise a fresh expedition for the exploration of what lies beyond. For frontiers of knowledge and capacity exist to be crossed ; and when every child shall be permitted to re-enter and, according to its share of the racial powers, to dominate its lost cosmical kingdom, we shall hear no more of barriers except the healthy ones of sanity, there, and ours, to bar out error alone : barriers that are themselves the very condition of really fruitful exploitation of reality, and so of yet further advance.

All this, then, applies to language, and to its temporary conditions and permanent tendencies. Once let us begin by a clear understanding of the true gist, trend, goal, and jurisdiction of expressive communication, and we enter a whole new world of power to discern and appraise, and thus to co-ordinate and act out of and upon, those realms of experience now most tragically arresting or misleading us.

Only, this fresh factor, this guiding concep-tion of what Language is, and must become, will need first to be applied in education.   When such an application really begins, much will have been gained besides more perfect communication in the linguistic sense.   We shall hear no more, then, of ability which might render the highest service to the race being wasted in routine work, or driven to suicide and even crime by sheer desperation induced by non-recognition of gift. Those now blind and dull to the unused human resources will have recovered a quick and keen sense, a racial sense, of the presence of these resources in unlikely directions—will, in fact, have been trained to look out for them—and will with this have evolved, in regard to the genuineness of claim to power of any kind, a much more discerning judgment than is yet possible, except in the rarest cases.

When the present state of things, as it has been vaguely and generally indicated in the preceding pages, is widely realised and admitted, it will be acknowledged that a radical regeneration of education, beginning in the nursery, is urgently called for.   As, however, this regenerated education will run with, and not as now against, a sanely broadening and deepening stream of effectiveness and human conquest in individuals and societies ; as it will mean, in fact, the application of normal powers now more or

less in abeyance or misused, and so will make
for a true solution of the most baffling problems
of life, there need be no misgiving as to its
ultimate effect.   And it will not be the least
merit of such an education, that, alone among
such ventures in the unknown, it will automatically furnish and bring to bear its own criticism,
which must needs be of the severest type we
know.   For speech and writing will be con-
ducted by a quickened and clarified intelligence,
using a linguistic instrument of immensely
enhanced delicacy and power, and therefore of
faithfulness at once to the cosmic reality and the
human intention.

XXX

MEANWHILE we have first to realise that to be inexpressive is for us the deepest of disgraces, involving the culpable neglect of our most precious power, the shameful disregard of our highest call. For all nature, all reality is expressive in an inexhaustible sense : but Man has the potency of a higher because an articulate and interpretative expressiveness. He alone reaches the level of the why and the because—inaccessible until the what and the how have been reached—and he alone can, if he will, raise this level to undreamt-of heights which are, even now, touched here and there by the hand of genius. But, except, perhaps, in the case of mathematics—and that only as separated off from the interests of all but specialised minds—and of the rare poetry which in the deepest sense should mean touch with the beauty, the honour, the divine grace, and the infinite range of truth, he misses as yet the noblest of all inheritances and the crown of his powers, that of the interpretative expression which is what many of us—vaguely or ambiguously or conventionally—call Revelation.

There is no veil over ineffable priceless Reality to be withdrawn : only over clouded human eyes.   One sees with reverence its reflection even now in the eyes less clouded than those of most of us ; in the eyes of the saint, the thinker, the worker ; above all, in the heavenly transparent simplicity of the true child's eyes.   All these *express* in their degree and at moments, and in so doing reveal.   But we allow what we call Expression, and especially that articulate language which should be our truest servant and greatest faculty, not merely to fail in revealing, but to mask and even falsify the urgent realities ever waiting for their appointed revealer.   We do not even yet know what Expression in its full compass might include and deliver to us.   But already we admit from time to time that some attitude or act, some gesture, or some change of these—all of them acknowledged lesser varieties of expressive resource—may, like some change of condition in natural objects, be profoundly suggestive and even explanatory.

Let us then resolve that articulate expression shall at last become worthy of Man, of one whose first duty and highest power is to interpret and thus to reveal ; whose prerogative it shall be to lay open to the pure eye of the candid and fearless because faithful mind, what are only secrets and mysteries to our ignorant sophistry and our often grotesque but enslaving belief.

For there is no ultimate difficulty. Truth is not innately mysterious. So far from trying to baffle us in order to enhance its command of us and keep us humble, as creatures of the ground ;[1] so far from inducing spiritual coma or delirium or dangerous obsession, Reality throws wide her blessed arms, opens wide all ways and paths which lead to her very heart, the heart of the Real. She asks only that the word of the enigma shall become a fitting word : that the expression of Man who himself is to *be* her expression shall be worthily 'incarnated' : that what is the very life-blood of man's thinking shall be enriched by purification : that in such a Word, while wealth of connotation and association may be boundless, a confusing or impoverishing ambiguity shall be reckoned as intellectual disgrace, as spiritual anathema.

And upon such a way let us bear in mind that Reality, our true goal, never breaks us up into rival, and thus mutually defeating and impotent, groups ; never creates cults which exclude a

[1] Latin *humilis* = of the ground, near the ground.

hundred types of humanity in order to dominate one. No; Reality groups, no doubt, but groups as our own organism groups the co-operating functions of its unified life : a type of grouping in which every system of parts serves every other faithfully and gladly. The life-current, the community of cells, the ramifying brotherhood of fibre, muscular and nervous : each adds to each other's power ; each is gladly servant of all other. And all ultimately unite in serving, and are as their great reward crowned by, a Brain as yet in the infancy of its conquests—a Brain which is there to cover the whole range of vital activities fully attained, embryonic, or still but potential.

Is any organic aim, indeed, yet fully attained ? Is the brain to generate its own superior ? Well, we know not. But at least we need not inflate Reality with our empty bladders of used-up thought, or shrink her into the wrinkled skin of decay. And to say 'we know not,' and for an unnecessary moment to rest content with that, is a crime against the Real around us and within us which calls in the most pleading, as the most commanding, of all voices.

Live in Me ; learn and know Me, saith all that is Real. *For the glamour or the horror of the Dream which haunts or fascinates, entrances or repels you—the adoration of false hopes, the cult of false despairs—shall vanish with the rising of my Sun, with the bearing and the birth of my being, as your true and waiting heritage.*

I open all: I keep back nothing: see that at least you learn to express me nobly, without flaw that need not be, or falsity that shames you, or blankness that defeats your highest powers. . . .

APPENDIX

" WE live in old cells, we move in old grooves, we go on using old watchwords, apparently unconscious that these are out of date and have lost their savour of meaning. . . . Do we not need a leaven of independent thought to make us distinguish what is from what has ceased to be real and essential ? . . . One is sometimes driven to conjecture that the faculty of independent thought is for the time weakened or distracted or numbed ; or may we hope and believe that the thought is there, and is only deficient in expression ? " (1)

" . . . language which is quite adequate in everyday life, language in which we describe ourselves as if we were things, living beings assigned to a particular time . . . that kind of language which is useful and legitimate for everyday purposes, becomes altogether misleading when we get to the problem of what is the true nature of reality. And the great difficulty which the metaphysician . . . has to face is just these incrustations of the everyday point of view, the language which we get into the habit of using, and the notions which pass current, and which give rise to what we may call superstitions of common sense based upon them, such as that the mind may be properly spoken of as a thing." (2)

" To what end led these ' new and fruitful physical conceptions ' to which I have just referred ? It is often described as the discovery of the ' laws connecting phenomena.' But this is certainly a misleading, and, in my opinion, a very inadequate, account of the subject. To begin with, it is not only inconvenient, but confusing, to describe as ' phenomena ' things which do not appear,

(1) Lord Rosebery, " On National Culture," October 15, 1901 (*Times* report). (2) R. B. Haldane, *The Pathway to Reality*, Series I. p. 40.

95

which never have appeared, and which never can appear, to beings so poorly provided as ourselves with the apparatus of sense perception. But apart from this, which is a linguistic error too deeply rooted to be easily exterminated, is it not most inaccurate in substance to say that a knowledge of Nature's laws is all we seek when investigating Nature?" (3)

"In the expressions we adopt to prescribe physical phenomena we necessarily hover between two extremes. We either have to choose a word which implies more than we can prove, or we have to use vague and general terms which hide the essential point, instead of bringing it out. . . . One of the principal obstacles to the rapid diffusion of a new idea lies in the difficulty of finding suitable expression to convey its essential point to other minds. Words have to be strained into a new sense, and scientific controversies constantly resolve themselves into differences about the meaning of words. On the other hand, a happy nomenclature has sometimes been more powerful than rigorous logic in allowing a new train of thought to be quickly and generally accepted." (4)

"Tous les observateurs sont aujourd'hui convaincus qu'il faut distinguer avec précision des réflexes cutanés ou tendineux, des réflexes inférieurs ou supérieurs, qu'il est puéril de confondre sous le même nom des amaigrissements et des atrophies, des tics et des spasmes, des secousses émotives et du clonus ; il faut se décider à comprendre qu'on ne doit pas davantage employer à tort et à travers les mots 'démonstration, persuasion, suggestion, association, idée fixe, etc.,' qu'il faut distinguer, dans les troubles de l'esprit, les idées fixes de telle ou telle espèce, les diverses formes de la conscience, les divers degrés de la dissociation psychologique.

"Cette précision du langage permettra seule de reconnaître nos erreurs inévitables, de comprendre mieux les malades, et de faire à la psychiatrie des progrès analogues à ceux qu'ont accomplis les études de neurologie. C'est cette analyse psychologique qui sera le point de départ des méthodes de *psychothérapie*. . . ." (5)

(3) A. J. Balfour's Inaugural Address as President of the Brit. Assoc., August 1904 (*Nature* report, August 18, 1904). (4) Professor Arthur Schuster, Brit. Assoc. (*Nature* report, August 4, 1892). (5) M. Pierre Janet, "Qu'est-ce qu'une Névrose?" (*Revue Scientifique*, January 30, 1909).

"Faraday . . . was obliged to explain the phenomena to himself by means of a symbolism which he could understand, instead of adopting what had hitherto been the only tongue of the learned." (6)

"Unfortunately we go on building with names when the things are altered or wasted away, as sometimes beavers pathetically persist in constructing dams and canals when the water has gradually dried up, or has changed its course. If we realise how a word may survive to oppress and mislead us, as other ghosts do, when the underlying thing has dissolved, we shall be more careful in setting up imposing names as we physicians are very prone to do, until we are sure that the thing is there ; and in no case shall we let a name give an absolute value to temporary or developing notions." (7)

"Ainsi la science n'est pas une œuvre de la nature, dont la conscience ne serait que le théâtre ; ce n'est pas non plus une simple provision de recettes, dont l'utilité serait toute la raison d'être. C'est une activité déterminée, c'est l'activité humaine elle-même, en tant que raisonnable et intelligente. Il en est de la science comme des langues. Ainsi que l'a finement démontré M. Bréal, les langues ne sont pas des êtres qui auraient leur principe d'existence et d'évolution en dehors de l'esprit humain. L'esprit, l'intelligence et la volonté humaine, voilà la seule cause vraie du langage ; et le langage ne saurait s'en détacher, parce qu'il n'y a de vie en lui que celle qu'il tient de cet esprit même." (8)

"C'est qu'il est impossible de donner une définition sans énoncer une phrase, et difficile d'énoncer une phrase sans y mettre un nom de nombre, ou au moins le mot plusieurs, ou au moins un mot au pluriel. Et alors la pente est glissante et à chaque instant on risque de tomber dans la pétition de principe. . . . Vous donnez du nombre une définition subtile ; puis, une fois cette définition donnée, vous n'y pensez plus ; parce que, en réalité ce n'est pas elle qui vous a appris ce que c'était que la nombre, vous le saviez depuis longtemps, et quand le mot nombre se retrouve plus loin sous votre plume, vous y attachez le même sens que le premier venu ; pour savoir quel est ce sens et s'il est bien le même dans telle phrase ou

(6) Clerk-Maxwell, *Scientific Papers*, vol. 2, p. 318. (7) Sir T. Clifford Allbutt on "Words and Things" (*The Lancet*, October 27, 1906). (8) Émile Boutroux, *Science et religion*, p. 279.

H

dans telle autre, il faut voir comment vous avez été amené à parler de nombre et à introduire ce mot dans ces deux phrases." **(9)**

"The indiscriminate confounding of all divergences from type into one heterogeneous heap under the name 'Variation' effectually concealed those features of order which the phenomena severally present, creating an enduring obstacle to the progress of evolutionary science. Specific normality and distinctness being regarded as an accidental product of exigency, it was thought safe to treat departures from such normality as comparable differences : all were 'variations' alike. . . . We might as well use one term to denote the differences between a bar of silver, a stick of lunar caustic, a shilling, or a teaspoon. No wonder that the ignorant tell us they can find no order in variation. This prodigious confusion, which has spread obscurity over every part of these inquiries, is traceable to the original misconception of the nature of specific difference, as a thing imposed and not inherent." **(10)**

"Within the cell-body are many collections, often in the form of granules, of substances which have not the protoplasmic attributes. They constitute the 'deuteroplasm' of certain cytologists. But these enclosed substances may be as far removed from protoplasm as starch grains. It is absurd to use the termination 'plasm' for such well-defined products of cell activity as these. The subject is, unfortunately, obscured by conflicting terms. Nomenclatures which were invented with the object of giving definiteness to our ideas have served but to perplex them. The term 'protoplasm' should be reserved as a synonym for the substance which is most alive, the substance in which chemical change is most active, the substance which has in the highest degree a potentiality of growth. Anatomical distinctions are better expressed in anatomical terms. We shall treat of such distinctions when considering the organisation of the cell." **(11)**

"No one can say what capacity living cells may have of taking substances from the blood, returning some of them, and excreting others. This unknown capacity leads to results which, when they do not appear to be in accordance with the laws of physics, are

(9) H. Poincaré, *Science et méthode*, pp. 166, 164-5. (10) Prof. W. Bateson, Brit. Assoc., August 1904 (*Nature* report, August 25, 1904). (11) Alex. Hill, *The Body at Work*, pp. 8-9.

commonly termed 'vital.' The term is a stumbling-block which has tripped up generations of physiologists." **(12)**

"Once upon a time there was a very bitter controversy as to the respective merits of Newton and Leibniz, in the discovery and elaboration of the infinitesimal method. Much of the dispute was due to the use of language appropriate only to the discrete aspects of quantity for the purpose of describing it when regarded as continuous." **(13)**

"The word 'instinct' is one of those unfortunate words which are supposed to be understood by all, words which are more fatal impediments to the advance of science than almost anything can be." **(14)**

"Malheureusement, nous sommès si habitués à éclaircir l'un par l'autre ces deux sens du même mot, à les apercevoir même l'un dans l'autre, que nous éprouvons une incroyable difficulté à les distinguer, ou tout au moins à exprimer cette distinction par le langage. . . . Nous éprouverions une surprise du même genre si, brisant les cadres du langage, nous nous efforcions de saisir nos idées elles-mêmes à l'état naturel . . . nous tombons inévitablement dans les erreurs de l'associationisme. . . . Aussi ne prennent-elles pas dans notre esprit la forme banale qu'elles revêtiront dès qu'on les en fera sortir pour les exprimer par des mots ; et bien que, chez d'autres esprits, elles portent le même nom, elles ne sont pas du tout la même chose." **(15)**

"Names lie nearest the surface of what we take for granted ; hence our difficulty in saying exactly what words, or ghosts of words, we have been using, and whether any." **(16)**

"I infer, therefore, that the pragmatic philosophy of religion, like most philosophies whose conclusions are interesting, turns on an unconscious play upon words. A common word—in this case, the word 'true'—is taken at the outset in an uncommon sense, but as the argument proceeds, the usual sense of the word gradually slips back, and the conclusions arrived at seem, therefore, quite

(12) Alex. Hill, *The Body at Work*, p. 205. (13) R. B. Haldane, *The Pathway to Reality*, Series I. p. 202. (14) J. Grote, *Exploratio Philosophica*, Part II. p. 3. (15) H. Bergson, *Essai sur les données immédiates de la conscience*, pp. 91, 101. (16) Prof. W. Mitchell, *Structure and Growth of the Mind*, pp. 372-3.

different from what they would be seen to be if the initial definition had been remembered." (17)

"No word has had more accusations of ambiguity, and consequently of unsuitability for scientific use, alleged against it than the word 'value.' Value in use, we are told, is one thing and value in exchange is quite another ; and that is unquestionably the case if we treat the phrases as museum specimens, if we put them each in its separate case and examine them there." (18)

"I avoid using the word 'soul' on purpose, because the endless confused controversy about it has rendered it, like many other words, unfit for use as a philosophical term, unless with constant accompanying definition." (19)

"The term 'Division,' which is the established designation of the procedure we have now to examine, is not happily chosen. We cannot appropriately speak of dividing a word, or the meaning of a word, for meanings are 'differentiated' rather than divided. The very term 'Division' (as also such other metaphorical expressions as 'parts,' 'joints,' etc.) seems almost to imply a physical division, a division of some individual thing into its component parts. The use of the word has the further disadvantage of prejudicing the interpretation to be put upon the process in its logical aspect." (20)

"It has clearly to be said that the definition of 'precocity' requires a little more careful consideration than it sometimes receives at the hands of those who have inquired into it, and that when we have carefully defined what we mean by 'precocity,' it is its absence rather than its presence which ought to astonish us in men of genius. . . . It is no doubt true that, in a vague use of the word, genius is very often indeed 'precocious' ; but it is evident that this statement is almost meaningless unless we use the word 'precocity' in a carefully defined manner." (21)

". . . tout homme qui réfléchit, est amené à faire en toutes choses, et sur laquelle repose, à vrai dire, toute vie, toute action :

(17) Bertrand Russell, *Philosophical Essays*, pp. 143-4. (18) W. W. Carlile, *Economic Method and Economic Fallacies*, p. 16. (19) J. Grote, *Exploratio Philosophica*, Part II. p. 3. (20) W. R. Boyce Gibson, *The Problem of Logic*, p. 40. (21) Havelock Ellis, *A Study of British Genius* pp. 136-7.

la distinction du principe et de l'application, de l'idée et de sa réalisation. Nous voulons avec notre pensée, nous réalisons avec les choses. Il s'ensuit qu'il y a, dans une action, dans une réalisation quelconque, quelque chose d'autre que la pensée, à savoir une forme matérielle, qui, si les conditions extérieures viennent à se modifier, devra nécessairement se modifier d'une manière correspondante, sous peine de changer de sens et de ne plus exprimer la même pensée. Pourquoi nos écrivains du XVIe siècle ont-ils aujourd'hui besoin d'explication, sinon parce que la langue a changé ? Pour dire aujourd'hui cela même qu'ils ont voulu dire, il faut souvent employer d'autres mots. Toute action, toute vie implique cette distinction, car la vie consiste à subsister au moyen du milieu dans lequel on se trouve ; et quand ce milieu change notablement, l'être vivant est placé dans l'alternative, ou d'évoluer, ou de disparaître." **(22)**

"Before I go further, I must guard against misunderstanding by a preliminary definition of terms. The name Monism is currently used indifferently to describe either of two very different doctrines, and it sometimes happens that the same person employs the word in both senses in the course of the same argument." **(23)**

"The ideas of right and wrong conduct are . . . those with which ethics is generally supposed to be most concerned. This view, which is unduly narrow, is fostered by the use of the one word *good*, both for the sort of conduct which is *right*, and for the sort of things which ought to exist on account of their intrinsic value. This double use of the word *good* is very confusing, and tends greatly to obscure the distinction of ends and means. . . . The word 'right' is very ambiguous, and it is by no means easy to distinguish the various meanings which it has in common parlance. Owing to the variety of these meanings, adherence to any one necessarily involves us in apparent paradoxes when we use it in a context which suggests one of the other meanings. This is the usual result of precision of language ; but so long as the paradoxes are merely verbal, they do not give rise to more than verbal objections." **(24)**

"In the exposition of mathematical thought the terms Number,

(22) Émile Boutroux, *Science et religion*, p. 243. **(23)** Prof. A. E. Taylor's contribution to Symposium on *Why Pluralism?* (Aristotelian Proceedings). **(24)** Bertrand Russell, *Philosophical Essays*, p. 16.

Quantity, Magnitude, and Measure, meet us at every turn. But while, in applied mathematics, writers who avoid looseness of terminology are careful to indicate, either by definition or by clear implication and example, the precise meaning which they attach to these terms, in pure mathematics it is a common if not invariable custom for writers to use these terms loosely, without any clear intimation of the shades of meaning intended, if any are intended." (25)

"What are purely descriptive principles in geometry? They are commonly understood to refer to qualitative relations, to exclude all reference to metrical relations. The investigation thus appears to start from, or to be founded upon, a contradiction. To establish the notion of distance upon principles which exclude this notion seems at first sight to be an absurdity. But it is only the phraseology which is absurd, because it does not express, in accordance with the usual conventions of language, the actual process of thought. The result of this violation of the conventions of expression is ambiguity in the doctrine itself. Hence the conflicting opinions which have arisen as to the significance of the theory." (26)

"First, I would draw attention to the simple yet pregnant facts, well established by the labours of philology, that the life of no single word is beyond the law of development—that finality in the significance of a word is never reached so long as that word continues to be used. Further, that the significance of a word depends ultimately not merely on the context, not merely even upon the whole treatise of which the context is a part, but finally on the whole of the rest of the language—and probably, in the last subtle analysis, it ends not even there. Now, if we remember that, ultimately, in a rigorously formal sense, definitions depend upon words, axioms depend upon definitions, and proof or reasoning upon axioms and definitions, it appears to be a simple and valid corollary that *axioms, definitions, and proofs never attain finality.* It may, indeed, be replied that this very argument—and, indeed, all arguments—assume implicitly the truth of the very axiom or principle the argument would question. But this objection,

(25) Hastings Berkeley, *Mysticism in Modern Mathematics*, pp. 60-61.
26) *Ibid.* p. 241.

ultimately analysed, is irrelevant, because the argument pretends to no higher degree of validity than the axioms upon which it ultimately rests. Whatever limitations may be discovered to apply to the one apply also to the other." (27)

" Europe had for centuries been filled with the noise of scholastic discussion over questions incomprehensible to ordinary sense, of which the staple was furnished by such terms as *substance, attribute, essence, existence, eternity.* And these terms were the established stock-in-trade, as it were, not only of philosophical language but of philosophical thought. Such as they were, these were the tools with which Spinoza had to work. Even if he could have conceived the notion of discarding them altogether and inventing new ones, which, however, was in his circumstances not possible, it was only by keeping them in use that he had any prospect of inducing students of philosophy to listen to him. But the powerful and subtle minds which had exercised themselves on these ideas had troubled themselves but little as to their relation to actual things and man's knowledge of them. It was assumed that the foundations had been settled once for all, while the flood of new ideas, unseen and irresistible, was in truth advancing to break them up. The cunningly wrought structure of mediæval philosophy was doomed ; and now that it has crumbled away, philosophy goes houseless, though not despairing ; for, after all, it is better to be a wanderer than to dwell in castles in the air.

" But meanwhile what was a man in Spinoza's place to do ? The terms were there to his hand, still the only currency of scholars ; the ideas for which they had been framed were dead or dying, and the great scientific conception of the unity and uniformity of the world, often seen as in visions, but now unveiled in all its power by Descartes, had already begun to spread abroad, subduing everything to its dominion. A sincere and unflinching eye could already see that in the end nothing would escape from it, not even the most secret recesses of human thought. Only in the light of this conquering idea could the old words live, if they were to live at all. If any vital truth lay hidden in them from of old, it would thus be brought out and bear its due fruit ; and what new life was wanting must be breathed into them through the new conception of the

(27) B. Branford, *A Study of Mathematical Education*, p. 314-15.

nature of things. This, I believe, was in effect the task Spinoza took upon himself. It cannot be maintained that it was altogether a possible one ; and it is at least doubtful whether Spinoza himself was fully aware of its magnitude." (28)

" We find in all human sciences that those ideas which seem to be most simple are really the most difficult to grasp with certainty and express with accuracy. The clearest witness to this fact is borne by the oldest of the sciences, Geometry. No difficulty whatever is found in defining a parabola, or a circle, or a triangle. When we come to a straight line, still more when we speak of a line in general, we feel that it is not so easy to be satisfied. And if it occurs to us to ask the geometer what is the relation of his 'length without breadth' to the sensible phenomena of space, matter, and motion, we shall find ourselves on the verge of problems which are still too deep for all the resources of mathematics and metaphysics together." (29)

" No tolerably prepared candidate in an English or American law school will hesitate to define an estate in fee simple : on the other hand, the greater have been a lawyer's opportunities of knowledge, and the more time he has given to the study of legal principles, the greater will be his hesitation in face of the apparently simple question, What is Law ? " (30)

" The commissioners recommend that the word 'lunatic' in the ordinary medical certificate be deleted and replaced by the words 'mentally defective person.' So far as comprehensiveness goes this is admirable. Whether it is a sufficiently accurate term to merit universal acceptance is another matter. There will, however, be general agreement with the resolution that the word 'lunatic' shall be henceforth discontinued as a descriptive term, that 'asylums' shall be called 'hospitals,' that the Board of Commissioners in Lunacy shall be called 'The Board of Control,' and that the term 'mentally defective' shall be defined in the proposed Act as comprising 'persons of unsound mind,' mentally infirm persons, idiots, imbeciles, feeble-minded persons, moral imbeciles, epileptics, and inebriates who are, mentally affected. It is only by such a radical change in nomenclature that the objects of including all these classes in one legal

(28) Sir F. Pollock, *Spinoza: His Life and Philosophy*, pp. 145-6
(29) Sir F. Pollock, *A First Book of Jurisprudence*, p. 3. (30) *Ibid.* p. 4.

category could be attained, though the definite term suggested may not, as has been hinted, be the most appropriate." **(31)**.

"The distinction made by the use of the term 'imprisonment' to denote sentences of two years and under, and penal servitude to denote sentences of five years and upwards, no longer has any significance now that they are both carried out in the United Kingdom; and it is misleading, for both classes of prisoners are undergoing 'imprisonment,' and are equally in a condition of penal servitude. The use of the term 'hard labour' in imposing the sentence of imprisonment, which is not used in passing one of penal servitude, might also well be omitted, for any prisoner sentenced to imprisonment should be and is by law required to labour under specified conditions suitable to his health and his capacity; and, in fact, except the specific kind of labour called first-class hard labour, defined in the Prisons Act, 1865, as crank, treadwheel, and other like kind of labour, the term 'hard' has no particular meaning, and its employment in the sentence makes no practical difference." **(32)**

"Clause 6 of the Land Bill. Somehow or other this clause had got into a terrible mess. There was a general consensus of opinion as to what was wanted; indeed, strange to relate, Mr. Balfour, Colonel Waring, and Mr. Healy were for once in accord, and Mr. Morley was not prepared to offer any substantial objection. But the difficulty was to devise a form of words which could be inserted in the Bill and be generally intelligible, and every member had his own ideas on this subject." **(33)**

(31) Report of the Royal Commission on the Care and Control of the Feeble-Minded (*Nature*, September 17, 1908). **(32)** Sir E. du Cane on "Convict Prisons," quoted in *Review of Reviews*, September 1896, p. 275. **(33)** *Daily Graphic*, May 9, 1891.

THE END

Printed by R. & R. CLARK, LIMITED, *Edinburgh.*

BY THE SAME AUTHOR.

Crown 8vo.   6s.

WHAT IS MEANING?

STUDIES IN THE DEVELOPMENT
OF SIGNIFICANCE

GUARDIAN.—" This volume is a plea for a thorough revision of our whole system of education, which fails, in the author's opinion, to lay the proper emphasis upon the question of ' Meaning, and how to convey it.'   It is a demand for a science of significs, which shall train us to see the importance of meaning and significance, and shall enable us to use language with a precision and exactness adequate to its importance as our main vehicle for expressing thought. . . . There is much in the book which is very suggestive, especially for those who are educational experts."

TIMES.—" Lady Welby has much that is interesting to say."

STANDARD.—" The little book is full of thought, knowledge, and observation ; and even those who do not accept, or may be unable to follow, the somewhat elaborate philosophic argument can appreciate the writer's wide range of illustration and allusion, and the ingenuity with which she presents her points. . . . Lady Welby displays so much learning and acuteness, and incidentally cites so many curious facts, that one reads her with unfailing interest.   The little book is most stimulating reading."

GLASGOW HERALD.—" An extremely thoughtful and suggestive book. . . . A wealth of illustration, an acuteness of observation, and an earnestness of purpose that are altogether admirable— the author well exemplifying in her own researches her definition in one place of ' significs ' as ' an unerring mental scent for the true sense of things.' "

MACMILLAN AND CO., Ltd., LONDON.

BY THE SAME AUTHOR.

Crown 8vo. 6s.

LINKS AND CLUES

SPECTATOR.—" It is a long time since we have read a book so full of the life of a true spiritual mind. . . . Indeed, it is not so much a book to read through, as to read and return to, as you do the Bible itself, from which its whole significance is derived in passages suited to the chief interest and difficulties of the moment. The author has lifted us into a phase of thought into which it is impossible for any one to enter without being convinced of the existence of the divine light. . . . We cannot too cordially recommend a book which awakens the spirit, as hardly any book of the last few years has awakened it, to the real meaning of the Christian life."

GUARDIAN.—" Is a valuable contribution to the literature of the spiritual life, and one which we trust will go far to fulfil the aspiration of its name, in these days of bewildering discord among Christians."

CHURCH QUARTERLY REVIEW.—" It seems hardly possible that these thoughts could have come from any mind which had not been trained and strengthened and taught by large and deep experience among a wide variety of human characters. . . . Lastly, though certainly not least, among the characteristics which must be noted throughout the book is the presence of a very keen and generous sympathy with every form of suffering and distress."

CHURCH TIMES.—" One of the most striking features of this original work is that while the greatest and deepest truths are approached from the intellectual side, the reader is raised into a high spiritual and devotional atmosphere ; the mind is called into energetic action, but in tones that also touch the heart and remind us that we are on holy ground. . . . *Links and Clues* is manifestly the result of deep thought and prayer, and . . . will well repay to the clergy and thoughtful laymen the time spent in a careful perusal."

MACMILLAN AND CO., LTD., LONDON.

14 DAY USE
RETURN TO DESK FROM WHICH BORROWED

LOAN DEPT.

This book is due on the last date stamped below,
or on the date to which renewed. Renewals only:
Tel. No. 642-3405
Renewals may be made 4 days priod to date due.
Renewed books are subject to immediate recall.

DEC

REC'D LD   DEC 2   70 -2 PM 2

Due end of WINTER Quarter   FEB 18 '71
subject to recall after —

IN STACKS   FEB 4 '71

REC'D LD   MAR 16 71 -6 PM 2
Due end of SPRING Quarter   APR 18 72
subject to recall after —

REC'D LD   JUN 12 72 -1 AM 4 8

APR 12 1985

REC CIR APR 15 1985

LD21A–60m-8,'70
(N8837s10)476—A-32

General Library
University of California
Berkeley